The Family of Faith

J. C. WENGER

HERALD PRESS
Scottdale, Pennsylvania
Kitchener, Ontario

THE FAMILY OF FAITH
Copyright © 1981 by Mennonite Board of Missions
     Elkhart, Ind. 46515
Published by Herald Press, Scottdale, Pa. 15683
          Released simultaneously in Canada by Herald Press,
          Kitchener, Ont. N2G 4M5
Library of Congress Catalog Card Number: 80-84609
International Standard Book Number: 0-8361-1951-7
Printed in the United States of America
Design: Alice B. Shetler/Art by Elmore Byler

81 82 83 84 85 86 10 9 8 7 6 5 4 3 2 1

Distributed overseas by Media Ministries,
Box 1252, Harrisonburg, Va. 22801

CONTENTS

PREFACE

Followers of Jesus Christ can be found today all over the world. Among these Christians are Mennonites who take their name from Menno Simons, a Frisian Reformer of the sixteenth century.

Until the nineteenth century, most Mennonites were found in Europe and North America. However, mission, relief, and service activities during the twentieth century have resulted in a worldwide Mennonite fellowship.

One major emphasis of the Mennonites is to practice in daily life the teachings of Jesus as found in the Bible. This book sets forth some of these teachings concerning the Christian church.

The Family of Faith is volume ten of the Mennonite Faith Series listed inside the book cover. The author, a lifelong student of the Scriptures and an ardent follower of Christ, shares helpful insights on the meaning of the church.

Believers who confess Jesus as Savior and Lord enter a new family, the family of faith. In this adopted family, they become one with many others "in Christ." And wherever they go they find mothers and fathers, brothers and sisters who love and care for them. Within this spiritual family, believers find help and strength to live the way taught by Jesus.

The references placed at the back of this book will assist the reader who wants to study further the biblical concept of the church and its message of hope for us.

—*J. Allen Brubaker*

ABRAHAM,
FATHER OF
THE FAITHFUL

ABOUT four thousand years ago in present-day Iraq lived a man named Abram. His city was called Ur, his country, Babylonia. Later God changed his name to Abraham, the common name for him in the Bible. He was married to Sarai (later Sarah), his half sister. Genesis 12 reports how God made Himself known to Abraham. God asked him to leave the highly civilized Ur and go to a country to which He would lead him. God promised to make of his family a great nation—now known as the Jews. God assured Abraham that through his family he would be a means of blessing to all the peoples of the earth.

Genesis 15 continues the story of God's favor toward Abraham. God assured him that he would have a vast multitude of descendants, although at the time he and Sarah did not have even one child. The narrative contains a key sentence: "Abram believed the LORD [Jahweh in Hebrew], and he credited it to him as righteousness" (Genesis 15:6). Abraham believed God before the child was conceived or born and obeyed God's call. Because of this faith and obedience, God considered him righteous. Abraham, therefore, came to be known as the father of those who have faith in God. From Abraham came the Old Testament family of faith. The people of God then, even in the Old Testament, came into being through faith in God's promises and in obedience to His call. Faith was the basis of righteousness rather than "being born of Abraham." Habakkuk (2:4) stated this truth clearly, "The righteous will live by his faith."

A Son Is Born

In due time—long after people normally bear children—Abraham and Sarah were favored with a baby son. When the LORD had promised Abraham and Sarah this son, they laughed. Therefore, the child was called Isaac, which in Hebrew meant laughter or "he laughs." God gave Abraham circumcision as a sign of the promise or covenant He had made with him. Henceforth this ceremony was to be performed on all baby boys when they were eight days old (Genesis 17:3-14).

The story of Genesis races on to the marriage of Isaac, and the birth of his twin sons, Jacob and Esau. Although both boys were sinful by nature, Jacob

6

(meaning "grasper" or "deceiver") turned to the Lord in true faith. Esau by nature and choice put little value on the things of God. The Book of Hebrews even calls him "godless" (12:16). In this spiritually dim age, Jacob had four wives who bore him twelve sons and a daughter. The twelve sons became the heads of the twelve tribes of "Israelites." God named Jacob "Israel" after he wrestled all night with an angel until he received a divine blessing. "Israel" means "he struggles with God."

Israel's Faith Is Tested

The country to which God led Abraham is now called Israel. In those days it was called Canaan. Isaac and Jacob lived there for many years. Jacob's eleventh son was called Joseph, a devout lad. God revealed to Joseph by dreams that he had a future of great power and glory. Joseph's brothers hated him for telling his dreams, and eventually sold him into slavery in Egypt. There, at the age of thirty, Joseph was able, with God's help, to interpret the dreams which troubled the Pharaoh, the king of Egypt. Pharaoh immediately made Joseph his chief ruler— what we could call the prime minister of the land.

Eventually, Joseph invited his father and his family to come to Egypt during a severe famine. God had foretold Joseph of the coming famine and so he had stored up vast amounts of grain to prepare for it. Years later a new Pharaoh came to the throne who did not remember Joseph. During his reign, the Egyptians made slaves of the Israelites.

God Delivers His People

After many generations had suffered the cruel

bondage of slavery, God heard their cry for deliverance. He raised up a leader named Moses, an Israelite who had been raised in the house of Pharaoh. Under God's direction and power, Moses led Israel out of Egypt, an event called the "Exodus."

In the Arabian desert, at the mountain called Sinai, God gave His law, the Ten Commandments. These moral teachings were given to guide the Israelites away from sin to a life of holiness and obedience. He also gave Israel a priesthood—the family of Aaron, the brother of Moses—to stand between God and the people.

God gave instructions for a sacrificial system in which animals were killed and their bodies offered to God as sacrifices for sin; God gave Moses detailed plans for a movable sanctuary, a sacred tent for worship. God directed that it should contain a holy place for religious ceremonies, and a most holy place or holy of holies in which to keep a sacred chest called the ark. It contained the Ten Commandments, written on stone tablets.

Israel's high priest sprinkled blood on the lid of the ark on the annual Day of Atonement to cover the sins of His failing people. The lid, therefore, was known as the mercy seat.

Israel Recites Her History

God chose Israel, not because they were better or greater than any other people, but only because of His great love for them (Deuteronomy 7:7-11). God told Israel through Moses, His spokesman, to recite her holy history as a regular part of her worship (Deuteronomy 26:5-10). The lights and shades of Israel's history were also recited in song—as in Psalms 105 and 106. This constant recital of God's faithful dealing with Israel was to help the nation remember His love for them—and that they were to play an important role in the salvation of all the peoples of the earth.

Only a Few Remain Faithful

Much of Israel's history is a sad story of disobedience to God's holy law. Israel's failure is recorded in Judges, Samuel, Kings, and Chronicles. But God always had His faithful remnant. The Book of Ruth sparkles with true faith and piety in a time of great spiritual darkness. Elijah, the prophet of God, thought he was the only man in Israel who still loved and served the Lord. However, God quickly assured him that He had a believing remnant of seven thousand persons (1 Kings 19:18).

This concept of the faithful remnant—the small body of true worshipers—became very meaningful to Israel's great prophets, the servants of the LORD. Many statements in the writings of Isaiah, Jeremiah, Ezekiel, Joel, Amos, Micah, Habakkuk, Zephaniah, Haggai, and Zechariah declare that God will show His faithfulness to the believing remnant of His people Israel.

The kingdoms of Israel and Judah were brought to ruin mostly because of sin and idolatry. Israel was exiled to Assyria in 722 BC, and Judah was exiled to Babylon in 605 and 586 BC. But God promised mercy to the believing remnant! He would provide a place of pasture for them; the LORD their God would care for them, and He would restore their fortunes (Zephaniah 2:7).

Malachi described the faithful remnant: "Then those who feared the LORD talked with each other, and the LORD listened and heard. A scroll of remembrance was written in his presence concerning those who feared the LORD and honored his name" (Malachi 3:16). This faithful remnant became a link to the new family of God in the New Testament or new covenant. Jesus Christ entered the world through this faithful remnant.

Blessed be the Lord God of Abraham, Isaac, and Jacob!

2

JESUS,
FOUNDER OF THE
NEW FAMILY OF FAITH

THE Gospel writers clearly linked the child Jesus, born in Bethlehem, to the faithful remnant of Old Testament Israel. Matthew and Luke trace Jesus' family line back to Abraham, the father of the faithful. Both writers show that Jesus' parents, Mary and Joseph, were strong in faith and lived uprightly. Both make clear that Jesus had no human father. He was conceived by the power of the Holy Spirit. The faithful remnant of the New Testament Israel accepted this miracle because of the references to it in the Old Testament. The unusual events surrounding the birth of Jesus also bore witness to the miracle of His conception (see Luke 1, 2).

This child was "God incognito." That is, He could not be recognized as divine through any external appearance. Nevertheless, the writer John says He was the eternal Son or Word of God (1:1). John states in 1:14 that the Word became a human being and "tented" among His people. This concept grows out of the experience of the Old Testament tabernacle. It was the tent in which the eternal God dwelled among His people. In Jesus, the eternal God was again dwelling among His people.

The life and ministry of Jesus were so important that the Western world began dating time from it. The ancient Romans used to date time from AUC. These letters stood for the Latin words meaning "from the founding of the city" [of Rome]. Jesus was born about the year 749 AUC, 5 BC in our calendar.

Jesus Grew Up Within the Faithful Remnant

The writer Luke tells us that Jesus was circumcised and presented to the LORD in the temple with a sacrifice, according to the law of Moses. We know very little of the childhood and youth of Jesus. Luke gives us one picture of Him in the temple at age 12. Luke also tells us that Jesus "grew in wisdom and stature and in favor with God and men."

John Prepared the Way for Jesus

John, the son of Zechariah and an important prophet of God, prepared the Jews for the ministry of Jesus. He preached strongly against sin and called for people to repent and to seal their repentance with water baptism. He, therefore, became known as John the Baptist.

Jesus Himself began His public ministry by accepting water baptism—evidently as a sign of Holy Spirit baptism. It was the Spirit who enabled Him to fulfill His ministry of teaching, healing, and preaching. The Spirit also enabled Him finally to die on Golgotha's cross. Each of the four Gospels point out that John baptized with water, but Jesus would baptize with the Holy Spirit. He also empowers the disciples of Christ to fulfill the ministry God calls them to and enables them to walk their Calvary road.

Christ Taught and Lived the Faith

Following His baptism and successful victory over the devil's temptations, Christ began His teaching ministry. "He taught in their synagogues, and everyone praised him" (Luke 4:15). His greatest summary of the will of God is found in what is known as the Sermon on the Mount (Matthew 5—7). Here Jesus explained the deepest intention of God for His children. His interpretation of the Old Testament contrasted sharply with the legalisms and weak explanations of the Jewish teachers of the day. "He taught as one who had authority" (Matthew 7:29).

Christ also went about doing good, showing what the Father is like in mercy, compassion, and power. His miracles of healing the sick, feeding the hungry, and showing love to the downtrodden were clear signs that He was the Messiah (or Christ, in Greek).

The Jewish Leaders Rejected Christ

Jesus' teaching and way of life clashed sharply with many of the views the Jewish teachers or rabbis held concerning God.

13

The Jewish leaders thought of God as a legalistic Judge, One who watches over His children with a critical eye. Jesus declared that God is a kind heavenly Father who loves us and provides for us; He is even to be called *Abba*, a warm family word in the Aramaic language used by the Jews of that era. It is something like Papa or Daddy.

The Jews interpreted the Old Testament in a very legal way. They said it contained 248 positive commands and 365 things we dare not do—a total of 613 rules! Jesus said that what God really wants is unselfish, warm love—love for God and love for people. Such love, said Jesus, enables people to become the kind of disciples God desires—without rules!

The Jews were always harping on good works. They were trying to earn the favor of God, trusting in prayers and alms especially. Jesus declared, "The work of God is this: to believe in the one he has sent" (John 6:29)!

The Jews thought they could earn access to God by merit and ritual. Jesus said that people should simply trust in the mercy and grace of God.

The Jews saw the Messiah as a great military leader who would free their nation and make them great. Jesus saw the Messiah as the suffering servant of Isaiah 53—a suffering and dying Lamb of God.

The Jews were proud to be the "seed of Abraham," and considered the Gentiles to be "dogs" in God's eyes. Jesus, however, declared that even the Jews needed to be "born again" (John 3). He had "other sheep" to be gathered into His one "fold" (John 10:16).

For the Jews nothing was more plain than the

right to fight for one's life. Jesus declared that unless a kernel of wheat falls into the ground and dies, it remains without fruit.

The Jews thought length and repetition added weight to their prayers; Jesus said that we should pray with joyful confidence.

The Jews considered it a mark of godliness to be harsh and severe with people who fail. Jesus saw it as godlike to forgive, to restore, to accept, and to love.

The Jews saw sin as a breaking of a code; Jesus saw sin as a heart condition crying for cleansing and renewal. Eventually the Jews called for the crucifixion of Jesus. To them, He was a hypocrite, a dangerous teacher, and an imposter.

Jesus Began a New Community of Faith

Matthew 16:13-20 tells us that Jesus looked forward to a new family of faith, His church or congregation. This new community of committed people *(ecclesia)* would be built on faith in Him. This new community would confess that He was the Messiah whom the prophets of old had foretold.

He declared that all the schemes of the underworld ("the gates of Hades" (would never be able to overthrow His community. Furthermore, His community would have ultimate authority to settle disputes between fellow believers (Matthew 18:15-17).

Jesus carefully laid the foundation for this new family of faith. From His many followers He carefully chose and taught twelve men who would later become the leaders of His church. The number twelve corresponds to the twelve sons of Jacob who headed the ancient Israel of God. An unknown writer put their names in a rhyme easy to remember:

Peter, Andrew, James, and John;
Philip and Bartholomew;
Matthew next and Thomas too;
James the Less and Judas the Greater;
Simon the Zealot and Judas the Traitor.

The Lamb of God Died for All

The shadow of the cross fell upon Jesus all through His ministry. He knew that as Moses hung a bronze snake on a pole, so He would have to hang on a cross (see John 3:14). He told the Jews that they could destroy His temple (body) and in three days He would again raise it up. On another occasion He commented that the "bread" which gave people life was His flesh which He would give for the life of the world. He would, He said, be staying on this earth for only a brief period. Then He would return to the One who sent Him.

Christ saw Himself as the Good Shepherd who would lay down His life for the sheep. When Judas objected to Mary putting costly ointment on Jesus, He said it was entirely proper; she was anointing Him for His burial. Three times He tried to tell His disciples that He would be killed by the Romans (Mark 8:31; 9:31; 10:33). Indeed, His purpose for coming into the world was to "give his life as a ransom for many" (Mark 10:45; Matthew 20:28). The epistles of the New Testament abound with references to the reconciliation with God which Jesus accomplished for mankind.

All Christ's words about His coming death were

fulfilled on Good Friday of Holy Week (AD 30). Unbelieving Jews in a moblike action persuaded the Roman governor of Palestine, Pontius Pilate, to sentence Jesus to death by crucifixion.

He Conquered Death

As Good Friday came to an end, a man named Joseph hurried to lay the body of Jesus in the tomb he had prepared for himself. The disciples rested on the Sabbath, according to the law. Then early on Easter Sunday the disciple Mary Magdalene and some women friends hurried to the tomb to put spices on the dead body of Jesus. To their great surprise, the stone was rolled back from the mouth of the tomb, and the body of Jesus was gone! Later Peter and John found the situation exactly as the women did.

Meanwhile, the risen Jesus began appearing to Mary, to Peter, to ten of the apostles, to the eleven (Judas, who betrayed his Lord had hanged himself). Finally, He appeared to over 500 brothers in the community of faith. Jesus appeared to the apostles (as the Twelve were known) to convince them that the prophets had clearly taught that the Messiah should suffer death, as He did, and then "enter His glory." Not only would the Messiah suffer as the Lamb of God, He would also "rise from the dead" on the third day. To convince His puzzled followers, He showed them the nail prints on His hands and feet, and even ate some broiled fish in their presence (Luke 24:13-48).

In His resurrected body, Jesus walked with two disciples on the Emmaus road and opened up the Scriptures to them as no man had ever done. So vivid was His teaching from "all the Scriptures" that their hearts were burning within them. Jesus' teaching ministry continued on with the apostles during the forty-day period between His resurrection and His ascension and enthronement at God's right hand. (For a fuller explanation of Jesus' life, ministry, passion, and resurrection, see *The Modern Student's Life of Christ* by Philip Vollmer, London and Edinburgh: Revell, 1912.)

Glory be to Jesus, the Lord of glory!

3

THE HOLY SPIRIT
EMPOWERS THE
PEOPLE OF GOD

BEFORE Jesus ascended to heaven, He told His
disciples that they were witnesses of His crucifixion
and resurrection. He told them to preach
repentance and forgiveness of sins in His name to all
nations, beginning at Jerusalem. Then He added,
"But stay in the city until you have been clothed
with power from on high" (Luke 24:46-49).

In chapter one of Acts the writer Luke repeats in
greater detail this same commission and instruction:
"Do not leave Jerusalem, but wait for the gift my
Father promised, which you have heard me speak
about. For John baptized with water, but in a few
days you will be baptized with the Holy Spirit"

(Acts 1:4, 5). He explained further: "You will receive power when the Holy Spirit comes on you; and you will be my witnesses in Jerusalem, and in all Judea and Samaria, and to the ends of the earth" (Acts 1:8). Then He ascended to the glory world.

Holy Spirit Baptism Occurs

Ten days later Christ's disciples gathered in Jerusalem for the festival known as Pentecost. This Jewish celebration was known in the Old Testament as the Feast of Weeks. It was celebrated on the first day of the week, fifty days after the beginning of the barley harvest. God therefore chose to "pour out His Spirit" upon His waiting community on a Sunday. This was the same day of the week that our Lord rose from the dead seven weeks earlier. This Pentecostal "baptism" was promised by various Old Testament prophets. Perhaps the most full prophecy is that of Joel as reported in Acts:

> And afterward,
> I will pour out my Spirit on all people.
> Your sons and daughters will prophesy,
> your old men will dream dreams,
> your young men will see visions.
> Even on my servants, both men and women,
> I will pour out my Spirit in those days (2:28, 29).

This outpouring of God's Spirit at Pentecost was a remarkable demonstration of God's presence and power. It was similar to God's use of wind and fire in the Old Testament to change a group of powerless slaves into a mighty nation. On the day God delivered His people Israel from Egypt, He caused a mighty wind to drive back the waters of the Sea of Reeds, an arm of the Red Sea. The trapped Israelites then escaped the pursuing army of Pharaoh by crossing on dry land. As they headed for the Promised Land, God used a pillar of fire to guide them at night.

In a similar way, God used wind and fire to give birth to the new community of faith at Pentecost. A sound as of a violent wind fell from heaven, and fire separated into what looked like "tongues of fire" and "came to rest on each of them. All of them were filled with the Holy Spirit and began to speak in other tongues [languages] as the Spirit enabled them" (Acts 2:2-4).

The Observers Are Puzzled

On this occasion Jews flocked in when they heard the sound of the wind. Although they came from possibly fifteen areas of the world, they all heard the Galilean believers speaking in their various native languages. "We hear them declaring the wonders of God in our own tongues!" they said. (No matter how great the miracle is, unbelief can always make a stupid comment. And so there were those who said this miracle came about by an excess of wine! 2:13.)

Peter Gives a Biblical Explanation

Peter, the Dean of the Twelve, stood up with the other apostles. With a vigorous voice he called on his fellow-Jews to listen to the true explanation. He declared that they had just witnessed a fulfillment of Joel's prophecy. Peter quoted at length from the prophet, closing with Joel 2:32:

And everyone who calls
on the name of the Lord will be saved.

Peter pointed out how God backed up the claims of Jesus with "miracles, wonders, and signs." He reminded them that they had handed Jesus over to the Romans to be crucified. "But God raised him from the dead"—as the prophets had foretold. Peter quoted Psalm 110:1, the Old Testament verse most often referred to in the New Testament. In this passage God said to Christ, the psalmist's Lord:

Sit at my right hand
until I make your enemies
a footstool for your feet.

On the basis of this, Peter declared firmly that "God has made this Jesus, whom you crucified, both Lord [Sovereign] and Christ [Messiah]" (Acts 2:36).

Many Repent and Believe

When the multitudes heard Peter's sermon, they were cut to the heart with Holy Spirit conviction. "Brothers, what shall we do?" they cried out to Peter and the other apostles.

Peter called on them to repent and to accept water baptism in the name of Jesus Christ for the forgiveness of sins. "And you will receive the gift of the Holy Spirit," Peter said. The response was indeed great, for 3,000 converts were added to the community of faith that happy day (Acts 2:37-41).

The New Israel of God Is Linked to the Old

Once again we observe that God here called a people for His name. This community was made up of those who walked in the way of faith, holiness, and obedience. And this family of faith was continuous with the believing remnant of Israel. Members of the community are therefore seen in the New Testament as children of Abraham, and as heirs of the promises made to the Old Testament patriarchs (Galatians 3:7; 3:29).

In their times Israel only was God's chosen people, His "priests," His holy nation, and a people for God's possession (Exodus 19:5, 6). Just so in the New Testament the new community of faith—believing Jews and Gentiles in one united body—is called "a chosen people, a royal priesthood, a holy nation, a people belonging to God.... Once you [Gentiles] were not a people, but now you are the people of God ..." (1 Peter 2:9). Believers from all nations of the earth are now included in the family of faith, the New Israel of God (Galatians 6:16)! All praise to "him who called you out of darkness into his wonderful light."

Jesus Prepares the Twelve

Jesus walked with and taught His Twelve apostles for possibly three years. Luke also notes that the Lord Jesus continued teaching them after His resurrection. His theme, Luke says, was the kingdom of God (Acts 1:3)—the "God Movement," as author Clarence Jordan has called it. The New Testament writers make clear that Jesus intended this God movement to find expression in local congregations. The Spirit of God led the apostles to carry out the "Great Commission" of our Lord by taking the good news to all the world. Much of the Book of Acts is devoted to this story.

The Church Calls Leaders

The Twelve served as Christ-appointed leaders, but local Christian congregations also chose elders. The selection of several elders in each congregation followed the synagogue system of leadership. And so the first missionaries appointed elders in each church—that is, in each new gathering of believers (Acts 14:23). (The Greek verb for appoint originally meant to elect by a show of hands, and Dr. R. F. Weymouth so translates it; the NIV however has "appointed" in the text, and "had elders elected" as another possible translation in the footnote.) The term elders in 1 Timothy 5:17 seems to be used for those who were also called overseers in Titus 1:7.

Those who served as pastoral assistants were called deacons (1 Timothy 3:8-13: Philippians 1:1). Romans 16:1 suggests that women may have served as deacons in the apostolic church. These congregational servants were also known by such general terms as presiders and leaders.

Some of the elders appear to have been primarily leaders and overseers, while others served as pastors and teachers (1 Timothy 5:17; Ephesians 4:11). The Holy Spirit gave some members, both men and women, the gift of prophecy. These prophets were free to speak out in the Christian assemblies. Indeed, all members were free to speak and teach (1 Corinthians 14:31). And the entire community of faith was told to "weigh carefully" the messages of the prophets (1 Corinthians 14:29).

Many women in the first-century church were illiterate. That may help to explain Paul's general rule that they should quit talking to their husbands and remain silent in the meetings (1 Corinthians

14:34-35). However, we do know that there were recognized prophetesses (Acts 21:9). The apostolic concern was that the family of faith, the church, might be strengthened and built up in the faith (1 Corinthians 14:1-12). All the gifts of the Spirit were to be used to that end.

Thank God for the ministry of the Spirit to us!

4

A CONVERTED PEOPLE

MEN and women of all nations enter the family of faith through a spiritual rebirth. *Repentance* and *faith* are two important aspects of this change, often known as conversion. Repentance means turning from sin. One of the most beautiful ways to describe a person's conversion is to say that he "turned to the Lord" (Acts 9:35; 11:21; 15:19).

Repentance, of course, means more than being sorry for the harvest of sin; it means being sorry enough to turn from sin to God. Faith means believing that what God says and does is true; it is personal trust in God. God has promised us salvation in Christ, and He accomplished that work on the cross.

Individual Experiences Differ

The self-righteous Saul was famous for the way he persecuted Christians. He thought he was doing God a service by having them beaten, put in chains, and jailed. However, he was shaken up when he learned that he was actually sinning against the risen and enthroned Christ. No wonder he went blind and fasted and prayed! (Read his conversion accounts in Acts 9, 22, and 26.)

The sinful woman who wept at the feet of Jesus expressed without words how sorry she was for the way she had lived. She was accepted and praised by the Lord (Luke 7).

Zacchaeus, a hard man who forced people to pay unduly large amounts of tax money, became rich. When he decided to follow the Jesus way of life he immediately gave half of his wealth to the poor. In addition, he made a 400 percent restoration to those he had cheated. (Read the story in Luke 19:1-10.)

Timothy was brought up as a son who early learned to obey his parents, to worship God, and to try to please Him. But he too had to commit his life to Christ. When we are first introduced to Timothy (Acts 16:1) he is already described as a disciple. Later he became one of Paul's most useful and loyal colleagues. Paul spoke most favorably of the true faith of Timothy's grandmother Lois and his mother Eunice (2 Timothy 1:5).

The Bible Describes Conversion

The Book of Acts contains many descriptions of people who were converted and thereby came into the church. Here are some of the many ways conversion is described:

Acts 2:41—Those who accepted his message were baptized.

2:47—The Lord added to their number [of the family of faith] daily those who were being saved.

3:19—*Repent,* then, and *turn to God* . . . .

5:14—More and more men and women believed in the Lord and were added to their number.

8:12—They believed Philip as he preached the good news of the kingdom of God and the name of Jesus Christ, [and] they were baptized, both men and women.

8:35, 36—Philip [told the Ethiopian] . . . the good news about Jesus. . . . And the [Ethiopian] . . . said, "Look, here is water. Why shouldn't I be baptized?"

9:35—All those who lived in Lydda and Sharon . . . turned to the Lord.

9:42—Many people [in Joppa] believed in the Lord.

10:44-46—While Peter was [preaching the good news of Jesus] . . . the Holy Spirit came on all [the relatives and friends of the Gentile Cornelius] who heard the message . . . . (And they were) speaking in tongues and praising God."

11:21—[At Antioch] a great number of people believed and turned to the Lord.

It would be a great experience to examine every case of conversion in the Book of Acts and in the Epistles of the New Testament. Try it!

Praise God that by His Spirit He continues to call people into the family of faith!

5

A FORGIVEN PEOPLE

THE Bible clearly teaches that the person who does wrong becomes guilty before God for what he has done. It is not merely that the sinner feels badly in conscience, he is really guilty in God's sight. He needs to repent of his sin and to take whatever steps are necessary to be forgiven. In the Old Testament, the one who sinned was to bring a sin offering to the priest, and confess his sin; when the sacrificial animal was killed, the blood "covered" or made atonement for his sin. Over and over the Old Testament declares, "In this way the priest will make atonement for him, and he will be forgiven" (see Leviticus 4:20, 26, 31, 35; 5:10, 13, 16, 18).

In the New Testament, Christ shed His precious blood for the forgiveness of the sins of the whole world. Now all the sinner needs to do is confess his sins to God, turn away from them, and believe in Jesus Christ as Savior and Lord. In the old covenant the priests offered sacrifices for the sins of the people day after day. But Christ "sacrificed for their sins once for all when he offered himself" (Hebrews 7:27). If animal sacrifices made people outwardly clean in the Old Testament era, "How much more, then, will the blood of Christ ... cleanse our consciences from acts that lead to death, so that we may serve the living God!" (Hebrews 9:14).

The Shedding of Christ's Blood Saves Us

The New Testament uses three expressions to emphasize that Christ's death on the cross saves us. When He shed His blood, He offered a sacrifice to God which was: (1) adequate for the salvation of all people, (2) offered to all, and (3) intended for all. He died for all, He shed His blood for all, and His cross makes possible the salvation of all.

The shedding of animal blood pointed forward to Christ's death, as Hebrews emphasizes. By His death, Jesus robbed Satan of his enslaving power (Hebrews 2:14) and made atonement for the sins of the people (Hebrews 2:17). Christ made peace with God through His blood (Colossians 1:20). And both Jew and Gentile were reconciled to God through the cross of Christ (Ephesians 2:16).

God Fully Forgives

"If we claim to be without sin, we deceive ourselves and the truth is not in us. If we confess our sins, he is faithful and just and will forgive us our sins and purify us from all unrighteousness" (1 John 1:8, 9). "Therefore, if anyone is in Christ, he is a new creation; the old has gone, the new has come! All this is from God, who reconciled us to himself through Christ and gave us the ministry of reconciliation: that God was reconciling the world to himself in Christ ..." (2 Corinthians 5:17-19).

The Community Forgives

When people repent of sin and turn to the Lord, the church is to warmly welcome them. All sins are to be fully forgiven and forgotten. The community of faith is not made up of people who have all been noble and pure; much more it is made up of people who, by turning to Christ in penitent faith, have been fully forgiven by God, *and by the people of God*. After a list of sins which banish people from the "God Movement," the Apostle Paul writes to the church at Corinth: "And that is what some of you were. But you were washed, you were sanctified [made holy], you were justified [pronounced righteous] in the name of the Lord Jesus Christ and by the Spirit of our God" (1 Corinthians 6:11). "Therefore, there is now no condemnation for those who are in Christ Jesus" (Romans 8:1).

Jesus had to drive seven demons out of Mary Magdalene (Mark 16:9), but after that she was just as much a part of the community of faith as the devout Lois and Eunice had been (2 Timothy 1:5)! It should be natural for one forgiven convert to fully accept another!

Let's forgive others as Christ forgives us!

6

A TRANSFORMED PEOPLE

WHEN a commander-in-chief of an army wins the decisive battle in a war, he looks forward with fresh courage and hope. The enemy has really been defeated, even though some small skirmishes remain. Some of those battles may be fierce, but the outcome of the war is now sure.

So it is with Christ and His family of faith, the church. It has to struggle with three great enemies—the world, the "flesh" (sinful human nature), and the devil. Christ won the decisive battle. He conquered those three enemies by His atoning death on the cross and His victorious resurrection from the dead. Victory for the church is sure, although sometimes its battles may be fierce indeed.

The New Testament Assures Victory

Christ's apostles knew that He had been victorious after they were filled with the Holy Spirit at Pentecost. On that great day they were empowered to face their Christian warfare. At times their battles with the powers of this world were really severe. For example, when the apostles were jailed for proclaiming Christ and His gospel. Or when James was beheaded. Or when Stephen was stoned to death.

Not the least of the enemies was Saul of Tarsus before he met the Lord on the road to Damascus. But the apostles were filled with deep joy and holy boldness as they saw the enthroned and omnipotent Christ putting down one enemy after another (1 Corinthians 15:24-28).

Not only has the decisive battle been won by Christ for His church; this victory may also be claimed in faith by each individual believer. Both present and past experiences make clear that Christians suffer the same human tragedies as non-Christians—health problems, financial setbacks, discouragement, fires, storms, the death of loved ones, and various kinds of failures.

However, no matter how dark life may seem, the believer looks forward in hope to the final victory Christ made possible through the cross. He won the decisive battle on that "green hill far away, outside a city wall"—on Golgotha just outside Jerusalem. The believer claims by faith the truth that no power on earth or hell can wrest him out of the Father's hand, for He is infinitely greater than any or all of the enemies (John 10:27-29).

The Believer Is Holy in God's Eyes

The Holy Spirit brings to an unconverted sinner pangs of conscience for his sin and creates in him a desire to be a child of God. This activity of God is spoken of as a "holy calling." The convert is urged by the Holy Spirit to make his "calling and election sure" (2 Peter 1:10). Because of the Spirit's work, the believer wants to unite with the holy community, the church of God in Christ. When he receives holy baptism with water he vows to live a life of faithful discipleship. He is to live, by God's help, a holy life.

In fact, as soon as he is converted he is called a holy person ("saint" in the English Bible). He may be a "babe in Christ," but he is now facing the glory world, having turned away from the sinful attractions of this wicked world. God therefore sees him as already holy!

The Believer Is Being Renewed Daily

Some Scriptures speak as if believers were already completely holy people. Other verses point out areas of partial defeat that call for further progress and victory. For example, Paul begins First Corinthians by declaring that the members of the church at Corinth were "sanctified ... called to be holy" (or "saints"). They were people who called on Christ, who had received the grace of God, who had been enriched in every way; they lacked no spiritual gift. They were eagerly waiting for Christ to return. He would keep them strong, so they would be blameless when He returned (see 1 Corinthians 1:2-9).

How surprising it seems when Paul warns them of the evil of party spirit in the church (Chapter 1), of the tragedy that they were still infants spiritually, actually worldly (3:1-3). Some were arrogant (4:18). There was undisciplined immorality in the church (5:1), as well as lawsuits between brothers in the family of faith (6:6), and more. In spite of all these tragic human failures Paul still kept his faith in the faithful God who had called them. Christ baptizes every convert with the Holy Spirit (12:13); and that Spirit is sure to chastise, correct, nurture, guide, bless, and fill each member of the holy community with divine love.

Paul's confidence was not in human nature, nor in the state of perfection of the church at Corinth. Rather, his confidence was in the faithfulness of God to bring each believer, no matter how weak, to full maturity in Christ. To this end Christ gives us gifts in the family of faith: apostles, prophets, evangelists, pastors, and teachers. Each of these spiritual gifts is intended to build up Christ's body to unity of faith and the knowledge of the Son of God, until we become mature, "attaining to the whole measure of the fullness of Christ" (Ephesians 4:11-13). Those who are in the church are not yet perfect, but they are pressing on toward the goal.

Our Confidence Is Total

The resources of Christ through the Spirit are adequate. His intention for us is glorious victory, even to the end. He will faithfully work in us so that we may "participate in the divine nature" (2 Peter 1:4). But Christians are urged again and again in the New Testament not to grow weary (Galatians 6:9; 2 Thessalonians 3:13), "not to receive God's grace in vain" (2 Corinthians 6:1), and not to "live according to the sinful nature," the flesh (Romans 8:13). Our part is to press on with Christ, to be obedient. The God "who began a good work in you will carry it on to completion . . ." (Philippians 1:6).

One of the most beautiful expressions of confidence is 2 Timothy 4:18: "The Lord will rescue me from every evil attack and will bring me safely to his heavenly kingdom. To him be glory for ever and ever. Amen."

Let's cling to this confidence!

7

A SHARING PEOPLE

SOME ROBBERS once approached a young farmer in Nebraska, pretending to be cattle buyers. When his wife went to town, they seized the farmer, tied him up, and hauled away his entire herd of beef cattle in two large trucks. The farmer was a member of a local Christian church. The members of his congregation and neighboring ones proceeded to follow the instructions of the New Testament. They dipped into their wallets and made up his loss. They lived out Christ's teachings and example.

Christ Our Example
Christ's love for mankind was so great that He

meekly laid down His life for our salvation. It's a rare event for a person to lay down his life—even for a righteous man; but Christ showed the greatness of His love by dying for the ungodly (Romans 5:6-8). His command to His disciples is that they show such love one to another (John 15:12, 13). Paul uses the healthy human body to illustrate how such love functions: every part labors for the welfare of the entire body. "If one part suffers, every part suffers with it ..." (1 Corinthians 12:26). Therefore he says, we are to carry one another's burdens, for in this way we "will fulfill the law of Christ" (Galatians 6:2). That is what Christianity is all about: showing love one to another! For that is how all people will know that we are Christ's disciples (John 13:34, 35).

When such mutual helpfulness is on an individual basis only, unequal sharing often results. Why? Because the need of one believer causes persons to respond with greater assistance than the need of another. There is good reason for believers to set up a systematic way to help members, especially in times of crisis such as fires, operations, tornadoes, and death. On such occasions, material aid is especially needed. Love and encouragement also provide a heart lift to the suffering member.

Mutual Aid, A Better Way

Society has many organizations to help people prepare in a systematic way for such events as illness, fires, storms, and death. But they are set up to make money. They solicit new members by promising security for oneself. The world says, "Every man for himself." But the family of faith says, "We must carry one another's burdens, and thus fulfill the commandment of Christ to show love one to another.

Justin Martyr wrote his *First Apology* for the Christian faith in the middle of the second century. He reports in clear, concise terms how the Christians helped and stood by one another: "The wealthy among us help the needy." Not to do so is a sin against Christ and His body, and is a witness against true Christian love. The heresy of the twentieth century is the notion that all one needs to do is confess Jesus—and then live as an individualist. The truth is that "salvation" (spiritual health, wholeness) is really found only as one becomes a caring member of the family of faith. Perhaps that explains the strange words of Justin, "We always keep together."

The life and welfare and witness of the community of faith is priority number one. This is the reason the Anabaptists advocated that the members of their severely persecuted congregations were to assemble several times a week. One of their much emphasized admonitions was: "Let us not give up meeting together . . ." (Hebrews 10:25).

Take No Interest from the Poor

The Anabaptists took seriously the law of love as set forth both by Jesus and the law of Moses. In the law it was forbidden to charge interest to a member of the covenant community: Exodus 22:25; Leviticus 25:36, 37; Deuteronomy 23:19. There are many similar references in the Books of the Prophets. Once again, the Christian disciple is to operate from the principle of sharing love, not selfish gain. This principle is to permeate all of the disciple's life.

How beautiful to live by Christ's law of love!

8

A WITNESSING
PEOPLE

CHRISTIANS of the twentieth century call the command to make disciples of all the nations (Matthew 28:18-20) the "Great Commission." This passage teaches that as Christians go into all the world, they are to bring to discipleship people from all the nations on earth; they are to create new communities of sharing faith and love. For Christ has "other sheep" which He wishes to gather into His fold, and there shall be one fold and one Shepherd (John 10:14-16).

Christian Witness Stifled
As early as the year 1526 a Latin phrase cropped

up in "Christian" Europe: *Cuius regio, eius religio* ("Whose the region, his the religion"). This meant the prince of each area chose whether he wished to follow the Lutheran, Reformed, or Roman faith; the creed and form of worship in his entire territory then had to conform to the religion he chose! This regrettable system went back to AD 380 and the supposed triumph of the Roman Catholic faith.

It was then that the Eastern and Western Emperors, Theodosius and Gratianus, made Catholic Christianity the official religion of the entire Roman Empire. Many Christians then and since have regarded that event as the "triumph" of the Christian faith. It was closer to the "fall" of Apostolic Christianity, for the "faith" was then forced upon people by law. Thereafter, dissenters were automatically in trouble, and there was no religious freedom or toleration. For example, the Donatists of the fourth century tried to exercise a stricter Christian discipline than their Catholic friends.

However, even the mighty Augustine, bishop of Hippo in North Africa, urged the state to use force against them. And rebaptism was made a crime punishable by death! Thus, the joining of church and state by the Roman emperors in fourth-century Europe led to the stifling of Christian witness.

New Testament Witness Revived

In sixteenth-century Europe the Anabaptists arose as they sought to be earnest disciples of Christ, Christians taking the New Testament as their sole guide. They claimed that most of the supposedly Christian populace of the so-called "Holy Roman Empire" were not, in truth, born-again disciples of

Jesus. Anabaptists, therefore, felt moved to go everywhere calling people to make the surrender of faith, and to seal their covenant of discipleship, even unto death if need be, with water baptism.

This angered the state church leaders, and they called upon the state to root out these radical Bible Christians by water, fire, and sword. This policy of persecution to the death was adopted at Speyer, a German city, in 1529, and was repeated in a later Diet at the same city, 1544.

Luther, the great Reformer, at first stood up bravely against the Catholics as he pleaded for toleration on the ground that his conscience was captive to the Word of God. Later, however, he vigorously opposed these free churchmen. This opposition is recorded in his writings, especially in the treatise, *Von den Schleichern und Winkelpredigern* (Concerning Sneaks and Hedge Preachers), 1532.

The Anabaptists believed that the family of faith was called to witness whenever possible to the glorious good news of salvation through Christ, a salvation which involved the keeping of the commandments of the New Testament. They went even so far as to convene a conference at Augsburg, 1527 (the so-called *Martyrs' Synod*), to plan how to share their renewed faith.

The group decided to send out witnesses all over Germanic Europe to share the gospel with all men, regardless of what happened to them personally. Many of these witnesses were captured and put to death as heretics. Their "heresy" was that they defied the right of the state to forbid evangelism, and that they believed in the baptism of converts rather than that of infants.

About 5,000 Anabaptists were executed in the first 75 years of the movement. This persecution caused the descendants of the Anabaptists to lose their vision of evangelism and missions—for some two and a half centuries! Since 1850 the vision has been slowly but steadily revived. Mennonites, who descended from the Anabaptists, are today widely scattered over the earth. They seek to establish everywhere spiritual "candles" for Christ and New Testament Christianity.

The Most Effective Witness

Many Christian believers do not fully grasp that the most effective witness to Christ is that of warm Christian communities of faith. In such communities no one lives for himself. Rather, all the believers live together in love and harmony. Each is more concerned for the welfare of the other disciples than he is for his own. These communities of deep love, holy joy, much sharing, and joyous mutual care would attract people from all classes of society by their "striking manner of life," as Christians were described in the second century *Epistle to Diognetus*.

Lord, help us all to be witnessing communities of love for the glory of Jesus!

9

A PEOPLE FROM
MANY NATIONS

GOD chose Abraham, Isaac, Jacob, and the twelve
tribes of Israel to be His special people, not because
they were better than other people, or greater in
number. Rather, the love of God, a love beyond
human comprehension, led Him to "elect" Israel to
be His special people (Deuteronomy 7:7-11). God's
purpose in choosing Israel was to make Him known
to all the peoples of the world.

Racism Twisted God's Election
God's election of the people of Israel placed a
great responsibility upon them. They were to give a
living and vital witness to God's special revelations

through the prophets from Moses to Malachi. Israel was to make known that there was but one God (the LORD), that He wanted a spiritual worship only (no images and idols), that He wanted a holy people who walked in righteousness and who did so out of a heart of love for Him.

But human nature led the Jews to think that they were in themselves better than other peoples. They became guilty of human pride—just as racial majorities in all parts of the world tend to look down on racial minorities. Such an attitude the Bible calls sin.

The Church, A Family for All Peoples

Christ announced clearly that He wanted a church that was open to all peoples. Before He returned to heaven forty days after His resurrection He told His disciples: "All authority in heaven and earth has been given to me. Therefore go and make disciples of all nations, baptizing them in the name of the Father and of the Son and of the Holy Spirit, and teaching them to obey everything I have commanded you. And surely I will be with you always, to the very end of the age" (Matthew 28:18-20).

Furthermore, the New Testament epistles quote Old Testament passages to show how God always intended to make the believing Gentiles "fellow heirs" with the believing remnant of Israel:

> Psalm 18:49—Therefore I will praise you among the
> Gentiles . . . I will sing hymns to your name
> (Romans 15:9).
> Deuteronomy 32:43—Rejoice, O Gentiles, with his
> people (Romans 15:10).
> Psalm 117:1—Praise the Lord, all you Gentiles, and

sing praises to him, all you peoples
(Romans 15:11).

Isaiah 11:10—The root of Jesse will spring up, one who
will arise to rule over the nations; the Gentiles will
hope in him (Romans 15:12).

The Church, A Mystery Revealed

Paul speaks of a "mystery" that has been through the ages at least partially locked in the heart of God. This "secret," revealed to Paul, was that the believing Gentiles should actually become one body, one family of faith, along with believing Jews. All peoples were, to be sure, lost in sin. But God in His great mercy has made believers alive with Christ; so we believers are saved by divine grace. With Christ we have co-ascended with Jesus and are even co-seated with Him in the "heavenlies"—so that in the ages to come He might show the amazing riches of His grace. On God's part we are saved by grace; on our part we lay hold of Christ for salvation by faith.

Christ took away the high wall of prejudice between Jews and Gentiles and made one new humanity of both groups. He did this when He died as a sacrifice for human sin, thus making peace with God for all believers—universally! Gentile believers are therefore now co-citizens with God's original special people, Israel. The church is in very truth the new "Israel of God" (Galatians 6:16).

The Local Church Reflects the Universal Church

As a young Christian, Peter may have been dimly aware of the intention of the Lord that His body, His people, should include believing Gentiles on exactly the same basis as believing Jews. Yet his

Jewish prejudice was so great that God had to show him the same vision three times. In the vision God told Peter to kill and eat animals which were ceremonially unclean. Peter naturally objected vigorously: "Surely not, Lord!" But God kept insisting that Peter was not to call anything unclean "that God has made clean."

Right after this, messengers came to ask Peter to come to the house of Cornelius, a Gentile living in Caesarea. Again the Lord spoke, telling Peter to go, "for I have sent them." Most amazing to Peter was the thing that happened in the house of Cornelius. While Peter was telling the gospel of Jesus to the family and friends of Cornelius, the Holy Spirit suddenly came upon them. Pentecost was repeated before the very eyes and ears of this still-prejudiced dean of the Twelve. But Peter was an honest disciple. Later he said: "If God gave them the same gift as he gave us, who believed in the Lord Jesus Christ, who was I to think that I could oppose God!"

When the Jewish believers at Jerusalem heard Peter's account of how it happened and why he baptized the believing Gentiles, they were satisfied. "They had no further objections and praised God, saying, 'So then, God has even granted the Gentiles repentance unto life'" (Acts 10:1—11:18). This was God's first step in taking believing Gentiles into the church.

The second step happened at Antioch, a huge city of Syria, north of Palestine. There nonresident Christian "missionaries" from Cyprus and from Cyrene in North Africa began to evangelize the Greeks. "And a great number of people believed and turned to the Lord" (Acts 11:19-21). And the process is still going on. For Christ by His Spirit is using His witnesses to make possible the glorious song revealed that the believers in Jesus, both

> You are worthy to take the scroll
>   and to open its seals,
>   because you were slain,
>   and with your blood you purchased men for God
> from every tribe and language and people and nation"
> (Revelation 5:9).

And in the final picture of the people of God, dwelling in the eternal city, the Apostle John reports that God's city had twelve gates. On the gates were the names of the twelve tribes of Israel. On the twelve foundations of the city were written the names of the twelve apostles of the Lamb. And their song revealed that the believers in Jesus, both Jewish and Gentile, were eternally one united and redeemed people of God for ever and ever (Revelation 21:9-14).

Now if the clear intention of God is to accept people from every tribe and nation, what a sin racial prejudice must be! This means that any congregation of the faithful, in any part of the world, should extend arms of love to those of other races and cultures. The one thing which makes a person a member of the family of faith is conversion from sin to Christ. Other factors do not count at all!

Lord, give us your vision of the church now and in the next world!

10

AN OBEDIENT PEOPLE

IN a May 30, 1525 letter (shortly after the first Anabaptists were baptized), Conrad Grebel, the Swiss founder of what is now the Mennonite Church, wrote: "For the doctrine [teaching] of the Lord and the commandments have been given for the purpose of being carried out and put into practice."

This sentence of Conrad Grebel pinpoints one of the chief emphases of the Anabaptist-Mennonite tradition. The Lord's Word is to be obeyed. And God is not satisfied with "selective obedience"; He wants full obedience. Christians cannot ignore the teachings of the New Testament that they do not like—rejecting such commands as "legalism."

Obey from a Heart of Love

The finest exposition of this biblical emphasis on obedience is the beautiful treatise of Michael Sattler. It was written in the first two years of the growth of the Anabaptist family of faith. Sattler, a former monk, was the outstanding leader in Switzerland after the death of Grebel in 1526 and Mantz in 1527.

Sattler's essay is called, "Two Kinds of Obedience." In it he says: (1) The obedience of a slave, a loveless conformity to the demands of the Lord, leads to a low level of performance. (It also produces proud Pharisees!) (2) The other kind of believers are people who love the Lord from the heart, who can never do enough in their desire to please Him. Such are the true children of God.

Obey the Scriptures, Test Tradition

The Roman Church had two sources of authority in doctrine: Scripture and tradition. The unwritten beliefs and customs handed down from one generation to another were held to agree with Scripture. But during the Middle or Dark Ages, tradition often became more authoritative than the Scriptures. The Reformer, Martin Luther, led out clearly in his great doctrine of *sola scriptura:* Only the Scriptures are the authority for faith and life.

"Willyam" Tyndale wrote one of the finest commentaries on the motive and strength for obedience. He was an English scholar burned at the stake for making a fresh translation of the Scriptures in English. Note in the following passage his emphasis on the work of the Holy Spirit. Tyndale's English of AD 1534 is so different from that of today that we will modernize his language, especially his spelling:

But now is the law spiritual, and no man fulfills it except that all he does springs from love, from the bottom of the heart. Such a new heart and strong courage toward the law, you can never come to by your own strength and power—only by the operation and working of the Spirit. For only the Spirit of God makes a man spiritual and like the law, so that henceforth he now does nothing from fear or for money or for the sake of advantage or for vainglory, but out of a free heart and from inward desire. The law is spiritual and will be both loved and fulfilled from a spiritual heart. Therefore, it necessarily requires the Spirit who makes a man's heart free, and gives him desire and courage in relation to the law. . . . To fulfill the law is to do its works, and whatever the law commands, with love, desire, and inward affection and delight; and to live godly and well, freely, willingly, and without the compulsion of the law—even as though there were no law at all. Such desire and free liberty to love the law comes only by the working of the Spirit in the heart. . . ."*

Tradition can help us to understand the past. However, it can block new workings of God's Spirit. Therefore, we should follow the Scriptures as our guide to faith and life. They will help us to evaluate tradition, to retain the good from the past and reject that which is not valid.

Avoid Legalism, Enjoy Freedom

Sincere Christians call for full obedience to the commands of Christ and His apostles. However, they do not ask for a cold-hearted legalism. Nor do

---

Prologue to Romans, pp. 295, 296 (1938 reprint of the 1534 New Testament, Cambridge University Press).

they call for the other extreme—defying the authority of the law of God (an error called *Antinomianism*). They stand with Michael Sattler and William Tyndale and many other sound teachers of the faith. They teach converted Spirit-filled people, out of love for God and mankind, to walk in all the commands of the Lord. This is the path of perfect freedom.

Their aim is to please God. Their model is the Lord Jesus. And their dynamic comes from the indwelling Spirit of God. They are not under law, but above law. What law could not do, God has done by sending His Son "in the likeness of sinful man" to be a sin offering. His sacrifice satisfied the righteous requirements of the law. Believers who walk not according to the "flesh" but according to the Spirit (Romans 8:2-4) can therefore live "free from the law." In Christ they live above the law.

Lord, so fill us with your love that we may joyously keep Your commandments.

11

A CELEBRATING PEOPLE

THE New Testament mentions several ways Christians celebrate their faith. Symbols standing for spiritual realities play a central role in these times of joy and happiness. Baptism and the Lord's Supper are two important occasions for celebration.

Christian Baptism

Little is known about the pre-Christian Jewish baptism of proselytes. We do know that such baptism celebrated the convert's new oneness with Israel, the people of God. The gospels, however, tell us plainly of the baptism of repentance which was practiced by John the Baptist. Finally, we come to

Christian baptism with water. It stands for the believer's new membership in the people of God, the family of faith. Baptism also shows that the one being baptized has *repented* of sin—has turned from the old life and entered a new one.

Water is often used to cleanse, and Christian baptism is a sign of the washing away of the guilt of sin. Most of all, baptism of the believer with water is a sort of mirror of how Christ baptizes His followers with the Holy Spirit. (He alone enables the new believer to live out the obligations of membership in the family of faith.)

By being baptized the convert also makes a covenant to walk faithfully as a disciple of Christ. It is a sign that one is ready to start down the "Calvary Road"—whatever it may cost to be a true disciple of Jesus. Baptism is also a commission, a sort of ordination, to serve as a witness to the good news of the gospel of Christ to a world lost in materialism, secularism, and carnality. In short, *baptism is a joyful celebration that the believer is now in Christ.*

The Lord's Supper

The second important celebration in the family of faith is the communion of the Lord's Supper. The broken bread and the "fruit of the vine," both humble elements, are rich in spiritual meaning! The broken bread reminds Christians that Christ redeemed them when His body was broken on the cross of Golgotha, a hill outside old Jerusalem. The cup reminds them of the blood Christ shed for the forgiveness of their sins. This forgiveness gives them "peace" (total well-being) with God and sets them free from the bondage of sin and Satan.

In the New Testament the loaf is also a symbol of the spiritual oneness and unity of those who are members of the family of faith. When a loaf of bread is baked in the oven, the individual grains are first pulverized, then the heat of the oven fuses them into one loaf, a single unit. So it is with the family of faith. The Spirit of God changes the individual believers into the image of their Lord, and thus binds them together in divine love. This line of thought is developed in the second-century *Didache* (the *Teaching* of the Twelve Apostles), in Augustine the North African bishop, and in Menno Simons of Friesland.

Writers, such as Conrad Grebel and Menno Simons, often spoke of the two ceremonies or the two sacraments. They meant baptism and the Lord's Supper, the two greatest celebrations of the Christian church.

A Service of Dedication

The common people came to love and trust the Son of Man in the days of His flesh. Some parents once brought their infants to the Lord for Him to bless them. The apostles undertook to send them away, thinking that Christ was too busy to bother with babies. But our Lord was much displeased. He called them back, took the infants in his arms, and blessed them.

He also pointed out that such children are in the kingdom (Mark 10:13-16). In fact He selected a child to answer to the question, "Who is greatest in the divine kingdom?" (Matthew 18:1-5). It is therefore in order for parents to bring their infants to their pastors for a prayer of blessing on the children. It is also in order for the parents to seek the help of the Lord and of the family of faith to give their children Christian nurture and training. These moments of blessing and commitment may take place in a service of dedication.

A Symbol of Service

Human rivalry was still in the inner circle of the Twelve about Jesus the night of His betrayal. To cleanse their hearts, Jesus laid aside His outer garments and girded Himself with a towel. He then stooped down like a servant and began to wash the feet of the Twelve. Peter felt keenly that such action was simply not appropriate on the part of his Master. He therefore objected strongly.

Jesus told Peter that His washing was essential if he was to belong to Jesus. Jesus also explained that he who has bathed is wholly clean. He needs only to wash his feet (when coming from the public bathhouse). Jesus here likens the new birth to a clean bath. He compares the washing of His disciples' feet to the daily cleansing the born-again child of God needs as he walks through this wicked world.

We do not know how widely the foot washing service was observed in early Christendom. Some Christian congregations in AD 200 observed the ceremony. Later the Synod of Toledo (AD 694) decided to require foot washing on the Thursday of Holy Week (called "Maundy" Thursday). Bernard of Clairvaux (1091-1153) saw it as a symbol of the Christian's daily cleansing. Dr. Balthasar Hubmaier observed it with his Anabaptist congregation as early as 1525. At that time most Anabaptists did not literally observe it as a congregational ceremony.

Later, perhaps partly through the influence of some of the Dutch Mennonites, foot washing slowly spread over parts of the worldwide Mennonite Church. Dirk Philips, a younger colleague of Menno Simons, saw two meanings in it: (1) as a symbol of the esteem in which we hold our fellow members in the body of Christ, and (2) as a symbol of the way Christ continually cleanses us in the inner man.

The Holy Kiss

For the first twelve hundred years of the Christian church, the holy kiss was observed on various occasions of church life. In the second century Justin Martyr describes its observance at the weekly meetings of the believers each "Day of the Sun" (Sunday).

In Mennonite circles it has been observed at baptism; at the installation of an elder, minister, or deacon; when pairs of men or women observe foot washing together; and when a member is reinstated after losing membership because of impenitence in sin—also as a warm greeting of love on various other occasions.

Other beautiful celebrations relate to marriage, the anointing of the sick with oil for divine healing, the commissioning of ministers for the service of the church, and the solemn and tender committal services at the grave before the burial of the dead.

Praise God for the meaningful symbols of the family of faith!

12

GOD'S PEOPLE, CITIZENS OF EARTH AND HEAVEN

THE people of God in the New Testament era are citizens of His heavenly kingdom and of an earthly state. Because they belong to two kingdoms they must keep clear which kingdom has the final authority over their lives. This is more difficult in New Testament times than it was during the Old Testament age.

Church and State Are One in Israel

God called the prophet Moses to lead His people out of the slavery of Egypt. His successor Joshua, son of Nun, led Israel into Canaan, the Promised Land. For many generations Israel then had no national government, just local leaders and judges. The latter served also as military deliverers from foreign oppression from time to time. During the last half of the eleventh century BC, Israel crowned her first king, Saul son of Kish, of the tribe of Benjamin. This choice of a king was contrary to the will of God. The prophet Samuel was deeply grieved that Israel wanted a king "like the other nations," for it was the LORD who wished to be their King.

Saul's successor was the devout David, "the sweet singer of Israel," and the "man after God's own heart." David reigned from about 1010 to 970 BC. When David's son Solomon died, the kingdom divided (about 931 BC) into the Southern kingdom of Judah and the Northern Kingdom of Israel.

Both kingdoms ended with foreign exile: Israel in 722 and Judah in 586 BC. Nevertheless, all through the kingship times Israel was guided somewhat by the LORD through His faithful servants, the prophets. (The real problem with Israel was the stubborn sin, idolatry, social injustice, and evil disregard of the warnings of Israel's prophets.)

In the first century AD a Jewish scholar named Josephus coined a term for the form of government which Israel had, at least partially. He called it a *theocracy*—that is, government by God. Thus, church and state were one in Israel.

All Peoples Need Human Governments
About 40 BC the Romans had finally managed to conquer the Jews and occupy Palestine. The Jews hated the Roman rulers with a vengeance. When Christ formally founded His church on the day of

Pentecost (about AD 30), He did not intend it to rule over the world. The church leaves to the governments of the many nations the functions of human government. These include keeping "law and order"—correcting lawbreakers and looking after the general welfare of the people.

Basic Contrast Between Church and State

One of the first Anabaptist documents to state this truth was the *Seven Articles of Schleitheim* (Switzerland), 1527. According to the Anabaptist-Mennonite understanding, the state includes all people, good and bad, while the church is made up of disciples of Jesus and their children. People enter the state by the natural birth, while full membership in the church comes through the new birth.

The state controls by law, while the church depends on the Word of God and the Spirit of God. The function of the state is to keep order in a "mixed society," and give as much justice to everyone as possible; the church is supposed to proclaim the gospel, to make disciples and baptize them, and to nurture its members in faith and holiness. The head of the state is a man or a group of men, while the Head of the church is the Lord Jesus Christ.

The state has such "sanctions" or penalties as fines and imprisonment. The church tries by loving affirmation and rebuke ("discipline") to restore the stumbling member; only with great regret may it finally use excommunication when there is a continuing refusal to repent. The human state will end when Christ returns, but the church will go with Him to the glory world for ever and ever.

God Controls History
Both the Old and New Testaments teach clearly that God rules over the nations of the earth, He oversees who is in control of their governments—in some cases to chasten, in others to bless. See Daniel 4 and Romans 13, for example.

Duties of Christians to the Government
Members of the family of faith show honor and respect to government authorities (Romans 13:7). In fact, the attitude of the Christian toward the authorities is to be one of meek submission (Romans 13:5; 1 Peter 2:13-17). This submission includes the payment of taxes and revenue (Romans 13:6, 7; Matthew 22:15-21). Most of all, it includes prayer "for kings and all those in authority" (1 Timothy 2:2).

Christians Witness to the Government
Mennonites believe in the free church principle. They hold that the government has no jurisdiction over the church. On the other hand, they believe the church has no right or power to order the government how to deal with criminals, pirates, or invaders. The church is asked to speak for God and His will. Therefore, God's family of faith may rightly urge upon the authorities the following considerations:

1. The state has no right to ask for divine honor and worship for its leaders.
2. The state has no right to crush political prisoners with cruel and inhuman punishments.
3. The state has no right to persecute religious

bodies of people for their religious convictions. Toleration of dissenters is right and proper.

4. The state should not use capital punishment. Only God, the Giver of life, has the right to end it (see Menno Simons, *Complete Writings*, pp. 920, 921).

5. The state ought not require Christians to violate their consciences. For example, commanding children of peace to kill in warfare. Nonresistant Christians are profoundingly grateful for the nations that now allow them to do work of national importance under civilian direction in times of war.

6. The church reminds national rulers that true security is from God Almighty; ever greater and more destructive armaments bring only more insecurity. The church asks the authorities to provide greater justice within the nation, better social conditions, greater opportunities for the poor and for racial minorities. The church warns national leaders against injustice, for it brings distress and turmoil within the nation. One reason for such injustice may be that too much attention is given to arms rivalry with other world powers. An important truth taught by history is this: nations do not generally collapse from a lack of military preparedness. Instead, they fall because of an inner erosion of their moral fiber. Woe to the nation that becomes completely secular, that allows homes to break down, divorces to become common, orphans to abound, crimes to flourish, and the church to be ill-treated. A vital church is a great help to the governing authorities. The spiritual renewal of John Wesley (1703-91) saved England from a costly, bloody revolution like that of the French (1789-99).

7. The state must be told clearly that it simply does not have the right or the authority to set aside the law of God. In the early centuries of the Christian era many infants were killed by their parents. This is called infanticide. And the early Christians quietly

insisted that infanticide was nothing less than SIN. Today the disciples of Christ must continue to insist that the planned destruction of human life is sin. No civil authority has the right or the power to set aside the law of God that human life is sacred. No parent has the right to destroy an unborn child, even in the early months of pregnancy. God is the Giver of life. See Jeremiah 1:5; Psalm 139:13-16. He only has the right to terminate life. (Medical conditions in the mother may force a surgeon to operate with the intention of saving at least her life, rather than to allow both mother and unborn infant to die. But most abortions are performed simply because the child is not wanted—and such intentional destruction of life is SIN.)

Dear Lord, help me to see my calling as a
Christian in relation to the state.
Enable all Christians to be "salt"
(a preservative)
and "light"
(making God's way of life clear).

13

GOD'S PEOPLE,
THE CHURCH
VICTORIOUS

CHRISTIANS view the history of the human race in eras. First is the time of no written law, from Adam to Moses (Romans 5:14). This is followed by the era of the law, from Moses to Christ (John 1:17). Third and final are the last days, the time from Christ's first coming to His return in glory (Hebrews 1:2; Acts 2:17).

Christ Is Coming as Judge
Many times in the course of His teaching ministry our Lord spoke of the day when He would come with power and great glory. Many of His sayings are brief, but there is one major description of the judg-

64

ment which He will hold: "When the Son of Man comes in his glory, and all the angels with him, he will sit on his throne in heavenly glory. All the nations will be gathered before him, and he will separate the people one from another as a shepherd separates the sheep from the goats. He will put the sheep on his right and the goats on his left.

"Then the King will say to those on his right hand, 'Come, you who are blessed by my Father; take your inheritance, the kingdom prepared for you since the creation of the world. For I was hungry and you gave me something to eat, I was thirsty and you gave me something to drink, I was a stranger and you invited me in, I needed clothes and you clothed me, I was sick and you looked after me, I was in prison and you came to visit me.'

"Then the righteous will answer him, 'Lord, when did we see you hungry and feed you, or thirsty and give you something to drink? When did we see you a stranger and invite you in, or needing clothes and clothe you? When did we see you sick or in prison and go to visit you?'

"The King will reply, 'I tell you the truth, whatever you did for one of the least of these brothers of mine, you did for me.'

"Then he will say to those on his left, 'Depart from me, you who are cursed, into the eternal fire prepared for the devil and his angels. For I was hungry and you gave me nothing to eat, I was thirsty and you gave me nothing to drink, I was a stranger and you did not invite me in, I needed clothes and you did not clothe me, I was sick and in prison and you did not look after me.'

"They also will answer, 'Lord, when did we see you hungry or thirsty or a stranger or needing clothes or sick or in prison, and did not help you?'

"He will reply, 'I tell you the truth, whatever you did not do for one of the least of these, you did not do for me.'

"Then they will go away to eternal punishment, but the righteous to eternal life" (Matthew 25:31-46).

Christ Will Raise the Dead

First Corinthians 15 outlines the triumphant return of Christ. The Apostle Paul sets forth first that which is "of first importance: that Christ died for our sins according to the Scriptures, that he was buried, that he was raised on the third day according to the Scriptures, and that he appeared to Peter, and then to the Twelve. After that, he appeared to more than five hundred of the brothers at the same time, most of whom are still living, though some have fallen asleep [died]. Then he appeared to James, then to all the apostles, and last of all he appeared to me also, as to one abnormally born" (1 Corinthians 15:3-8). Paul's first point here is the *fact* of Christ's resurrection.

Then Paul turns to the order of events when Christ returns: "Christ has indeed been raised from the dead, the firstfruits of those to have fallen asleep [died]. For since death came through a man [Adam], the resurrection of the dead comes also through a man [Christ]. For as in Adam all die, so in Christ all will be made alive. But each in his own turn: Christ, the firstfruits; then, when he comes, those who belong to him. Then the end will come, when he hands over the kingdom to God the Father after he has destroyed all dominion, authority and power. For he must reign until he has put all his enemies under his feet ..." (1 Corinthians 15:20-25).

The Nature of the Resurrection Body

"But someone may ask, 'How are the dead raised? With what kind of body will they come?'"... When you sow, you do not plant the body that will be, but just a seed, perhaps of wheat or of something else. But God gives it a body as he has determined...."

Paul then makes a number of contrasts between the body laid in the earth and the resurrection body:

Present body	1 Corinthians	Resurrection body
1. Perishable	15:42	1. Imperishable
2. Dishonor	15:43	2. Glory
3. Weakness	15:43	3. Power
4. Natural	15:44	4. Spiritual
5. Likeness of Adam	15:49	5. Likeness of Christ
6. Flesh and blood	15:50, 51	6. Changed

"I declare to you, brothers, that flesh and blood cannot inherit the kingdom of God, nor does the perishable inherit the imperishable [world]. Listen, I tell you a mystery [divine secret]: We will not all sleep, but we will all be changed—in a flash, in the twinkling of an eye, at the last trumpet. For the trumpet will sound, the dead will be raised imperishable, and we will be changed....

"Therefore, my dear brothers, stand firm. Let nothing move you. Always give yourselves fully to the work of the Lord, because you know that your labor in the Lord is not in vain" (1 Corinthians 15:50-52, 58).

The Great Separation When Christ Returns

"Brothers, we do not want you to be ignorant about those who fall asleep, or to grieve like the rest of men, who have no hope. We believe that Jesus died and rose again and so we believe that God will bring with Jesus those who have fallen asleep [died] in him. According to the Lord's own word, we tell you that we who are still alive, who are left till the coming of the Lord, will certainly not precede those who have fallen asleep.

For the Lord himself will come down from heaven, with a loud command, with the voice of the archangel and with the trumpet call of God, and the dead in Christ will rise first. After that, we who are still alive and are left will be caught up with them in the clouds to meet the Lord in the air. And so we will be with the Lord forever. Therefore encourage each other with these words.

"Now brothers, about times and dates we do not need to write to you, for you know very well that the day of the Lord will come like a thief in the night. While people are saying, 'Peace and safety,' destruction will come on them suddenly, as labor pains on a pregnant woman, and they will not escape.

"But you, brothers, are not in darkness so that this day should surprise you like a thief. You are all sons of the light and sons of the day" (1 Thessalonians 4:13—5:5).

The Bliss of Heaven: The Church Triumphant

"Then I heard what sounded like a great multitude, like the roar of rushing waters and like loud peals of thunder, shouting:

'Hallelujah!
For our Lord God Almighty reigns.
Let us rejoice and be glad
and give him glory!

For the wedding of the Lamb has come,
and his bride has made herself ready.
Fine linen, bright and clean,
was given her to wear.' "

The bride is the church. Fine linen stands for the righteous acts of the saints which adorn the church (Revelation 19:6-8).

What Christ's Return Does for Us Now

"Dear friends, now we are children of God, and what we will be has not yet been made known. But we know that when he appears, we shall be like him, for we shall see him as he is. Everyone who has this hope in him purifies himself, just as he is pure" (1 John 3:2, 3).

Lord, by your Spirit make this hope vivid in our hearts!

FOR FURTHER READING
AND STUDY

Harold S. Bender. *These Are My People*, Herald Press, Scottdale, Pa., 1962

Ross T. Bender. *The People of God*, Herald Press, Scottdale, Pa., 1971

Donald F. Durnbaugh. *The Believers' Church*, Macmillan N.Y.; Collier-Macmillan, London, 1968

James Leo Garrett, Jr., Editor. *The Concept of the Believer's Church*, Herald Press, Scottdale, Pa., 1970

Marlin Jeschke. *Discipling the Brother*, Herald Press, Scottdale, Pa., 1972

C. Norman Kraus. *The Community of the Spirit*, Eerdmans, Grand Rapids, Mich., 1974

Franklin H. Littell, *The Free Church*, Starr King Press, Beacon Hill, Boston, 1957

_____*The Origins of Sectarian Protestantism: A Study of the Anabaptist View of the Church*, Macmillan, N.Y.; Collier-Macmillan, London, Second Printing, 1968

Lesslie Newbigen. *The Household of God*, SCM Press, London, Third Printing, 1955

Ernest A. Payne. *The Fellowship of Believers*, Carey Kingsgate Press, London, 1952

P. K. Regier *et al. Proceedings of the Study Conference on the Believers' Church*, General Conference Mennonite Church, Newton, Kan., 1955

Wilbert R. Shenk, Editor. *The Challenge of Church Growth: A Symposium*, Herald Press, Scottdale, Pa.; Kitchener, Ont., 1973

J. N. Smucker, *et al. Studies in Church Discipline*, Mennonite Publication Office, Newton, Kan., 1958

Gunnar Westin. *The Free Church Through the Ages*, Broadman Press, Nashville, Tenn., 1958

J. C. Wenger is professor of Historical Theology in Goshen Biblical Seminary, a school of the Associated Mennonite Biblical Seminaries, Elkhart, Indiana. He has made a lifelong study of Anabaptism and has published numerous articles and books in the field.

He studied at Eastern Mennonite and Goshen colleges (BA), at Westminster and Princeton Theological seminaries, and at the universities of Basel, Chicago, Michigan (MA in Philosophy), and Zurich (ThD).

He has taught at Eastern Mennonite and at Union Biblical (India) seminaries, and has served on the Committee on Bible Translation which prepared *The New International Version*.

He is a member of the Evangelical Theological Society. He has served on the editorial boards of the *Mennonite Quarterly Review*, of *Studies in Anabaptist and Mennonite History*, and of *The Mennonite Encyclopedia*, and on the executive council of the Institute of Mennonite Studies.

He has served the Mennonites as a deacon, a minister, and a bishop. He has been a member of their Historical Committee, Publication Board, Board of Education, district and general conference executive committees, and of the Presidium of the Mennonite World Conference.

He married the former Ruth D. Detweiler, RN, in 1937. They are the parents of two sons and two daughters.

A familiar sight in his home city of Goshen is J. C. riding his bicycle on a local errand.